The Inventor's Spark

Five Marvelous Stories of People Who Helped Shape the Modern World

Nury Vittachi
Illustrations by Step Cheung

Contents

THE BOY WHO COMBINED A BIKE AND A TRAIN TO INVENT THE CAR

LITTLE KARL REMEMBERED almost nothing about his father. The boy was only two years old when the man had died.

But his mother Josephine spoke about him.

"Your father was a train driver," she said. And she would show him the big, powerful, steaming locomotive trains that existed in those days.

Karl and his mother had a hard life. They had no money. But she instilled values in him, and encouraged him to study hard and be ambitious.

STEP C

Karl Benz, who was born in 1844 in Germany, did so well in his studies that when he was nine, he was sent to a science school called the Lyceum. From there, while still in his early teens, he studied at the Poly-Technical University.

In those days, there were no planes or cars, and rich people travelled in horse-drawn carriages.

Poor people like Karl would just walk, or, if they were lucky, they would ride bicycles.

One day, while riding his cheap old bicycle to school, he had a thought. What if you could build an engine, something like what existed in one of his father's trains, but really, really small — so small, that you could put it into a carriage or even onto a bicycle?

It would be like a tiny little, one-person train — a horseless carriage!

Although he was training to be a locksmith, he decided to change course and study locomotive engineering, and follow the steps of his much-missed father.

At the age of 15, Karl managed to get into a big university to study mechanical engineering, and afterwards worked as an engineer for various companies.

But he was still thinking about his mini-engine idea, and when he was 28, he started to become more entrepreneurial.

Encouraged by his new wife, a lively girl called Bertha, he invented different mechanisms, such as an ignition system, spark plugs, a gear shift and all sorts of things that you would need to have in the "horseless carriage" of his dreams.

When he found a friend who ran a bicycle repair shop, everything came together. Using wire wheels from bicycles and other elements from the engines he had invented, the first car was born: The Benz Patent Motorwagen.

It looked like a big tricycle, but it moved by itself just fine, and could take you up and down the street. You didn't need a horse, and you didn't have to pedal! It was astonishing.

Karl's wife Bertha believed that it could do more than go up and down the street to amazed looks: it could take people long distances. So, without telling him, she borrowed it and took their children with her — using his machine to drive out of the city to visit relatives.

The trip was a great success — and the age of cars had begun.

If Karl Benz's train-driving father was looking down from heaven, he would surely be proud of his son, the inventor of the car.

THE FAILED DOCTOR WHO SPARKED AN IDEA

YOUNG JOHN WALKER PROBABLY felt like a failure.

He was given a job as an assistant to a surgeon at the age of 15. His parents hoped he would become a doctor himself.

But he hated most things about it: the illnesses and the unhappy people, and the difficulty of knowing whether you were helping or harming people.

So he gave up the profession.

Instead, he made a quiet job for himself doing the one part that he did like. He became a chemist, mixing medicines and selling them from a small shop in the UK. This was in the early 1800s.

One day, he became intrigued by a puzzle. There were so many things you could make instantly — you could turn powder into drinks, or sand into cement. Was there a way to instantly make fire?

Fire is such an important and useful thing that humans had been dealing with this question for a long time. More than a million years ago, a type of early man called Homo erectus was making fire the old way, rubbing sticks together, or making sparks by smashing pieces of a rock called flint together. Modern humans, Homo sapiens, often still used the same method, generating sparks to light things.

Making fire took a long time, it was tiring, and did not always work.

In China, around the year AD 950, a man had the idea of soaking little sticks with chemicals that made them flammable.

If you wanted to light a fire quickly, you could get some flints and try to make sparks which would set the little "fire inch sticks" alight.

It made the process slightly quicker, but not much. You still had to spend a long time trying to create sparks.

By the 1800s, people in Europe were trying to find quicker ways of making fire. Some carried chemical sticks plus a bottle of a dangerous chemical to dip them in, which would cause them to burst into flames.

In another method, chemicals were wrapped in a glass bubble which was wrapped in paper and you had to smash it (some people did it with their teeth) to get the chemicals to mix and burn.

All the methods were tricky, inconvenient and dangerous.

John Walker tried to mix chemicals together too, to see what happened. One day, he got a blob of something very sticky on the end of a long stick. He scraped it along his stone floor to try to get the blob off.

Instead, it burst into flames.

John Walker had invented the first convenient match. All you had to do was scrape it along a rough surface and it would instantly change from being a cold, dry stick of wood to being a live flame.

Most of the doctors who were alive at that time have been forgotten.

But the man who felt like a failure is in the history books as the inventor of friction matches, one of the most successful inventions of modern history.

THE WOMAN TO THANK IF YOU LIKE CHOCOLATE

MARY HAD A PROBLEM in her cauldron. She was an alchemist.

In movies and books, alchemists are often presented as wizards, but they were often just good chemical scientists, as Mary was.

For her latest experiment to work, she had to take a substance and heat it to a high temperature for a long time. She had to make it melt to produce the potion she needed.

But every time she tried it, the same thing happened. Just as the melting process began, the edges of the substance would start burning. It quickly ended up as a blackened lump stuck on the bottom of the cauldron. It was so frustrating!

STEP C.

How could she solve this problem? There was nobody to ask, because she was one of the first of her kind — this happened a looong time ago.

Alchemists should be thought of as very open-minded early scientists. They were interested in physical and chemical reactions, but were also open to blending in a bit of magic if they felt like it.

If their ancient book said that the experiment worked better if done in the noon sunshine of mid-summer's day while chanting a certain spell, they would try it that way, and sometimes it did seem to make a difference.

Historians don't know much about Mary except that she was a Jewish woman who lived somewhere in Europe about AD 150.

She was also known as Miriam Prophetissima and Mary the Jewess and was very respected, since she was believed to be the first alchemist in the Western world.

Until she came along, the East had several examples of this type of chemical experimenter, but the West had produced a different sort of scientist (particularly in Greece), who were more philosophical, and who focused on the principles of physics, mathematics, and other areas.

So Mary was a pioneer. And she was smart.

She soon worked out that the answer to this problem, as with many science problems, was to find (or in her case, create) the right equipment. She did quite a lot of this. Some historians say she may have invented a distillation system and a vapor collection system during her experiments.

But most importantly, it does seem that she solved the puzzle of finding a way to make a fierce heat work in a gentle, consistent way, melting without burning, to turn solids into liquids without turning them into blackened lumps.

If you want to understand her problem, you could put some chocolate into a microwave oven. All ovens are different, but most people who do this will find that some parts of the chocolate start to melt, while other parts harden and burn.

To solve the problem, Mary made a two-level cauldron, the bottom one filled with boiling water and the top one containing the substance to be melted.

Water always boils at 100 degrees Celsius, and no more. It is not like fire, which can just get hotter and hotter. The two-layer arrangement, with the fire heating the water, and the water heating the thing that needed to be melted, worked perfectly.

The fire could continue to burn, heating the bottom cauldron, but the top cauldron would never go above 100 degrees Celsius.

It caused melting without burning, and spread to alchemists around the world. It became known as a "bain-marie" (which is French for "Mary's bath").

Today, you can find bain-maries in all chemistry labs. But they are even more common in kitchens around the world. That's because you need a bain-marie to melt chocolate, so that you can shape it or use it to coat things, making yummy snacks and desserts!

The next time you eat anything that is chocolate-covered, spare a thought for Mary, the West's first alchemist, puzzling over her cauldron 18 centuries ago.

THE MAN IN THE BURNING HOUSE

IF SOMETHING NEEDED TO be fixed at the rich man's house, a staff member would call "the handyman".

Except the handyman wasn't a man at all — he was a dark-skinned boy of 16.

His name was Garrett Augustus Morgan, and he was the son of slaves who married and had children when slavery was abolished.

But though they were not still slaves (this was in the 1890s), they were poor, the boy had little education, and they had to work long hours.

Yet there was one handyman job he really liked: fixing the sewing machine.

Sewing machines were complicated in those days. You pushed a hanging platform with your feet, and through a bicycle-like system of gears, it made the machine at the top perform its sewing functions.

Garrett become so good at this that when he was in his 20s, he started his own sewing machine repair shop in the American city where he lived.

He realized after a while that when he fixed machines, what he was really doing was the science of engineering — understanding how things are supposed to work and making them work better.

So he became an inventor.

One day he noticed that people who died in house fires usually did not burn to death, but died from inhaling smoke.

He knew there was still air in the rooms in which they were trapped. Smoke rises, so there was clear air at floor level.

Garrett Morgan designed a hood with long, dangling tubes. You could move through a smoke-filled room in a burning house and breathe quite well, since the air came from ground level.

But people just didn't believe that a young black man could invent clever, useful things.

So he paid for an actor, who was not black, to pretend to be the inventor. Garrett himself would pretend to be the assistant, and he would don the hood and enter a tent filled with poisonous smoke to demonstrate how it worked.

One night in 1916 he was fast asleep when a messenger arrived at his house.

There had been an accident in a tunnel deep underground. "Bring your masks," the runner said.

Garrett and his brother rushed to the scene. Workers had been overcome by smoke in a tunnel, and the people who had gone down to rescue them had not come out.

The inventor and his brother used the masks to save the rescuers and bring out the bodies of the victims.

Today, people are trained to know that if they are trapped in a burning place, they should put a wet towel around their heads and drop to the ground to breath the air at floor level.

If you do that, you are kind of creating a Garrett Morgan hood, so say a word of thanks to the handyman who saved lives with it 100 years ago.

THE BOY WHO LOST HIS CHANCE BUT GOT IT BACK

SOMETIMES YOU GET ONLY one opportunity in life — and someone snatches it away.

That was the sad story for a hard-working boy called Gregorio Zara.

He lived in the town of Lipa in Batangas, the Philippines, and there was not much chance of advancement there.

Except for one thing. There was ONE school prize available. The top performer at high school would get a scholarship to travel to the USA and study there.

It would be just what Gregorio needed. He was a very smart child, but came from a humble family who had no hope of sending him to a fancy university overseas.

STEP C.

Gregorio studied hard all the way through his primary school and high school and succeeded in becoming the top student in the town.

But bad news followed. A high official had demanded that the prize go to a different student.

Gregorio got nothing.

He and his family dealt with the disappointment and he instead went to enroll at a local university.

But some weeks later, there was some surprising news. The person who had taken the scholarship had been taken ill and died.

Most of the scholarship money had not been spent, and would be given to Gregorio Zara after all. He was going to be an international scholar!

He went to the USA and then to France and quickly became a famous inventor.

He patented many inventions, but one of the most interesting was an early videophone. Way back in 1955, people were still getting used to ordinary telephones, and the idea of a videophone was very futuristic. He called it the "photo phone signal separator network".

But even though Gregorio and other inventors had worked out how to send and receive pictures in phone conversations so long ago, it wasn't until 2006, when many people had computers with the Skype program on them, that video calls become easy, cheap and popular.

Gregorio Zara was a successful scientist and could easily have stayed in the West. But he chose to come back and live in his home country, the Philippines.

He also discovered the law of electrical kinetic resistance, now called the Zara effect, and created early solar-powered devices. Back home, he married a beauty queen, Engracia Laconico, who was Miss Philippines at one time, and they had four children.

Today, when cartoonists draw pictures of scientists, they often draw a European man in a white coat with Einstein hair. Actually, Einstein never wore a white coat and stayed away from laboratories!

And if you take a look at history, you find that discoverers, both male and female, came from every culture in the world.

Gregorio Zara died in 1978. If there's such a thing as the after-life, it would be lovely to have a video-phone conversation with him and see what he thinks of all the Skype-like conversations we have these days!

KEEP READING

READING ABOUT THE LIVES of scientists and other discoverers adds to our store of knowledge, but we hope also leads us towards something much greater, which is wisdom.

This book is part of a series, which we hope you'll enjoy reading, and will spur you on to do your own scientific research.

The creators of this book wish you success in your explorations.

THE YOUNG SCIENTISTS SERIES

Book 1: SECRETS IN THE ROCKS
Five Astounding Tales of People Solving Mysteries Beneath Our Feet

Book 2: FABULOUS PHYSICS
Five Amazing Stories of People Who Solved Nature's Puzzles

Book 3: MAGICAL MATHEMATICS
Five Astonishing Stories of People Who Did Miracles with Numbers

Book 4: BREAKERS OF BARRIERS
Five Stunning Stories of People Demolishing Walls to Make History

Book 5: SCIENTIFIC PIONEERS
Five Incredible Tales of People Who Helped Develop the Scientific Method

Book 6: THE AMAZING QUANTUM
Five Awesome Stories of People Who Made a Revolution in Physics

Book 7: THE SCIENCE OF HUMANITY
Five Fascinating Stories of People Who Helped Us Understand Ourselves

Book 8: WOMEN OF DISCOVERY
Five Super Stories of Fabulous Females Who Made Scientific History

Book 9: THE INVENTOR'S SPARK
Five Marvelous Stories of People Who Helped Shape the Modern World

Book 10: ADVANCES IN ALCHEMY
Five Startling Stories of Chemistry and Biology

Book 11: THE CALL OF THE STARS
Five Wonderful Stories of People Looking to the Heavens

Book 12: MYSTERIES OF NATURE'S LAWS
Five Striking Stories of People Investigating the Deepest Puzzles of Reality

Published by

WS Education, an imprint of
World Scientific Publishing Co. Pte. Ltd.
5 Toh Tuck Link, Singapore 596224
USA office: 27 Warren Street, Suite 401-402, Hackensack, NJ 07601
UK office: 57 Shelton Street, Covent Garden, London WC2H 9HE

National Library Board, Singapore Cataloguing in Publication Data
Name(s): Vittachi, Nury, 1958– | Cheung, Step, illustrator.
Title: The inventor's spark : five marvelous stories of people who helped shape the modern world / author, Nury Vittachi ; illustrator, Step Cheung.
Other title(s): Young scientists series ; 9.
Description: Singapore : World Scientific Publishing Co Pte Ltd, 2017.
Identifier(s): OCN 969706097 | ISBN 978-981-3221-64-2 (paperback)
Subject(s): LCSH: Scientists--Juvenile literature. | Inventors--Juvenile literature. | Science--Juvenile literature. | Inventions--Juvenile literature.
Classification: DDC 509.22--dc23

British Library Cataloguing-in-Publication Data
A catalogue record for this book is available from the British Library.

All royalties received will be channelled to the National Book Development Council of Singapore (NBDCS) as a gift from the author.

First published 2017
Reprinted 2018

Printed in Singapore